DRUMS

Senior Author
William K. Durr

Senior Coordinating Author
John J. Pikulski

Coordinating Authors
Rita M. Bean
J. David Cooper
Nicholas A. Glaser
M. Jean Greenlaw
Hugh Schoephoerster

Authors
Mary Lou Alsin
Kathryn Au
Rosalinda B. Barrera
Joseph E. Brzeinski
Ruth P. Bunyan

Jacqueline C. Comas
Frank X. Estrada
Robert L. Hillerich
Timothy G. Johnson
Pamela A. Mason
Joseph S. Renzulli

HOUGHTON MIFFLIN COMPANY   BOSTON

Atlanta   Dallas   Geneva, Illinois   Palo Alto   Princeton   Toronto

Contents

3	**A Good Home**	Laurene Krasny Brown
11	Skill: **Plurals**	
12	**Think Big!**	Joan Lynn Carbonali
22	**Boo Bear and the Kite**	David McPhail
31	Skill: **Contractions**	
32	**A Big Surprise**	Joan Lynn Carbonali
42	**Things That Go**	Reading for Information
45	Skill: **Predicting Outcomes**	
46	**Fox Gets Lunch**	James Marshall
56	**Reading Helps**	

ART CREDITS
ILLUSTRATION: 3-10 Marc Brown; 11 Diane Palmisciano; 12-21 Pamela Johnson; 22-30 David McPhail; 31 Diane Palmisciano; 32-41 Dora Leder; 45 Diane Palmisciano; 46-55 James Marshall; 56 Andrzej Dudzinski, Ellen Walsh
PHOTOGRAPHY: 42 (top left) Jim Pickerell; (bottom left) Joe DiMaggio/Peter Arnold; (bottom right) Lee L. Waldman/Earth Images; 43 (top left) Alan Oransky/Stock Boston; (top right) Hank Morgan/Rainbow; (bottom) Coco McCoy/Rainbow; 44 (top right) Bohdan Hrynewych/Southern Light; (middle left) Diane Koos Gentry/Black Star; (bottom) Rob Nelson/Picture Group; (inside back cover) Macy Lawrence and Associates
COVER, TITLE PAGE: Stella Ormai

Copyright © 1989, 1986 by Houghton Mifflin Company. All rights reserved.
No part of this work may be reproduced or transmitted in any form or by any means, electronic or mechanical, including photocopying and recording, or by any information storage or retrieval system without the prior written permission of Houghton Mifflin Company unless such copying is expressly permitted by federal copyright law. Address inquiries to Permissions, Houghton Mifflin Company, One Beacon Street, Boston, MA 02108.
Printed in the U.S.A.
ISBN 0-395-43677-X

CDEFGHIJ-D-943210/89

Come in, Bear.
Take a look in here.

I see! I see!
Do you want me to help you?

I do not think you can help me.
But I think Turtle can.
I will go to see Turtle.

 What can I do for you?

 I would like to find a good home.
Can you help me, Turtle?

 I can help you, Rabbit.
I will take you to see a home now.

What a big home!
Do you like this home, Rabbit?

I do like it.
But it is too big!
This is not the home for me.

 I have the home for you, Rabbit.

 Take me to it, Turtle!

 Now this is a good home!

 It is a good home for a bear.
But it is not good for a rabbit.
I want to get out!

 I will find a good home for you.

Do you like this home, Rabbit?

I can not get in it!
What will I do now, Turtle?
I have to find a good home!

I can not help you, Rabbit.
You do not like what I have.

 I will help you, Rabbit.

 I would like help, Bear.
But what can you do for me?

 You will see what I can do.

I want to see, too.
I do not think Bear can help.

 What do you think now, Turtle?

 You did help, Bear.
Good for you!

 What do you think, Rabbit?

 I think I like it here.
This is the home for me!

Skill Plurals

What Do I Have?

Think Big!

by Joan Lynn Carbonali

Ana: We will have fun here, Pam.

Pam: We can have fun, Ana.
But I do have work to do.
I want to see what bears are like.

Ana: I like bears.

Pam: I do, too.
Bears are big.

Ana: I can help you do your work.

Pam: You can not do this work, Ana.
But you can help me.
You can help me find the bears.

Ana: The bears are in here.
But look, Pam!
We can not get in.

Pam: Now what will I do?
I can not see the bears.

Ana: You can work in here, Pam.
This is where the turtles are.
You can see what turtles are like.

Pam: I want to see bears, not turtles.
Turtles are too little.

Ana: Take a look here, Pam.
This is where the rabbits are.
You can do your work here.

Pam: I do not want to work here.
Rabbits are too little for me.
Turtles and rabbits are too little!

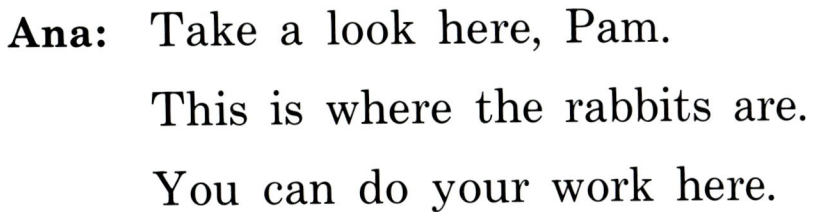

Ana: This is where the cats are.
I see little cats and big cats.
Would cats be good for your work?

Pam: The big cats would be OK.
I will look here.

Ana: Now this is big!
It is not a bear.
But Pam will like this!

Ana: Pam! Pam!

Come and see this animal!

Pam: Did you find a bear, Ana?

Ana: I did not find a bear.

But you will like what I did find.

Pam: This is big!
I like this animal!
I will work here!

Ana: See, Pam.
I did help you.

Pam: You are a big help, Ana.
Now I can get to work!

Boo Bear
and the Kite
by David McPhail

Boo: Do you like this kite, Pig?

Pig: It is a good kite, Boo.
I want to see it fly.

Boo: OK, Pig. I will fly the kite.
It will be fun.

Pig: Go, Boo, go!

Boo: This is not fun, Pig!
I can not make the kite fly.

Pig: I can get your kite to fly.

Boo: What a good friend you are!
You take the kite and fly it.

Pig: OK, Boo. Look out!
Here I go!

Boo: Go, Pig, go!
Make my kite fly!

Pig: I can not do it, Boo.
Your kite will not fly.
It is not a good day to fly a kite!

Boo: Here comes my friend Fox.
Fox will make my kite fly!

Fox: Good day, Boo and Pig.
This is a good day to fly a kite.
Kites are fun.

Boo: It is not a good day for my kite.
My kite will not fly.

Fox: I see what you need.
You need a big tail.

Pig: I have a tail.
But my tail is little.

Boo: My tail is little, too.

Pig: We can not fly the kite, Boo.
We do not have big tails.

Boo: You have a big tail, Fox.
You will have to fly my kite.

Fox: You do not need a big tail, Boo.
The kite needs a big tail!
We can make a tail for the kite.
I think we have what we need.

Boo: Now I see, Fox!
Now we can fly my kite!

Fox: Go fly the kite, Boo and Pig!
You can do it now.

Pig: This will be fun!

Boo: The tail works, Fox.
See my kite go!
What a good day to fly a kite!

Skill Contractions

Where Is My Friend?

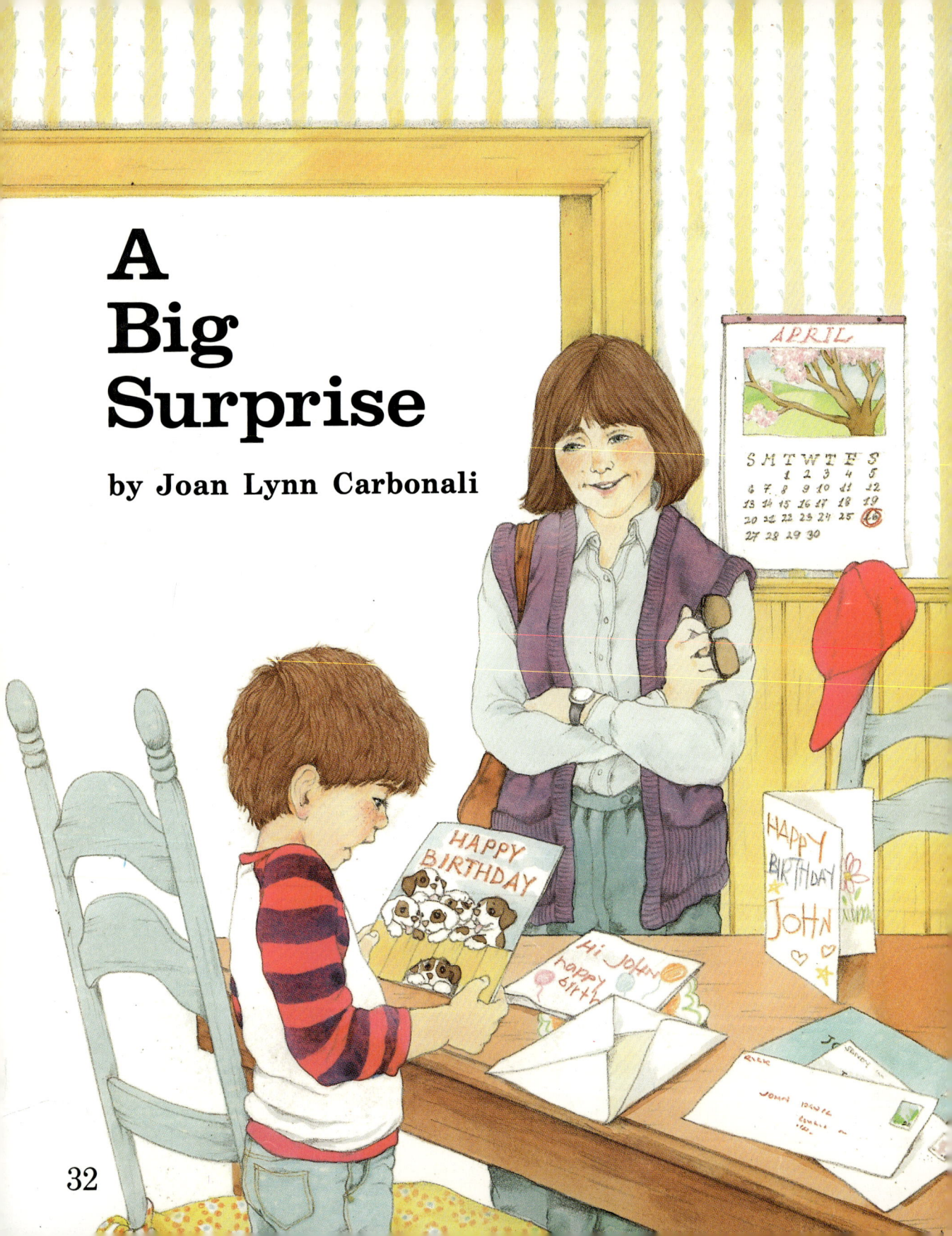

A Big Surprise

by Joan Lynn Carbonali

Mother: This is your big day, John.
I have a surprise for you.

John: I like surprises, Mother!
Where is my surprise?

Mother: Your surprise isn't here.
We have to go out for it.

John: I want Gramps to come, too.
Where is Gramps?

Mother: Gramps is at work, John.
Gramps can't come.

John: This is my big day, Mother.
I would like Gramps to be with me.

Mother: Look, John.
This is where Gramps works.

John: Can we see Gramps at work?
It's fun to surprise Gramps.

Mother: I think Gramps would like that.
Gramps likes surprises.

John: I like it here, Mother.
Some day I want to work here.
I want to fly like Gramps.

Mother: Some day you may do that, John.
You would be good at it.

John: I see Gramps now!
Surprise, Gramps!

Gramps: This is your big day, John.
What will you do?
Where will you go?

John: Mother will not tell me.
It's a surprise, Gramps.

Gramps: Surprises are fun.

John: My surprise will be fun.
It would be more fun with you.

Gramps: I would like to be with you, John.
But I have some more work to do.
Go with your mother and have fun.

John: What is my surprise, Mother?

Mother: I can't tell you that, John. It would not be a surprise!

John: May I look now, Mother?

Mother: OK, John, now you may look!

John: My friends are here!

Mother: Here's your hat, John.
Your friends have hats.
You need a hat, too.

John: This will be fun!

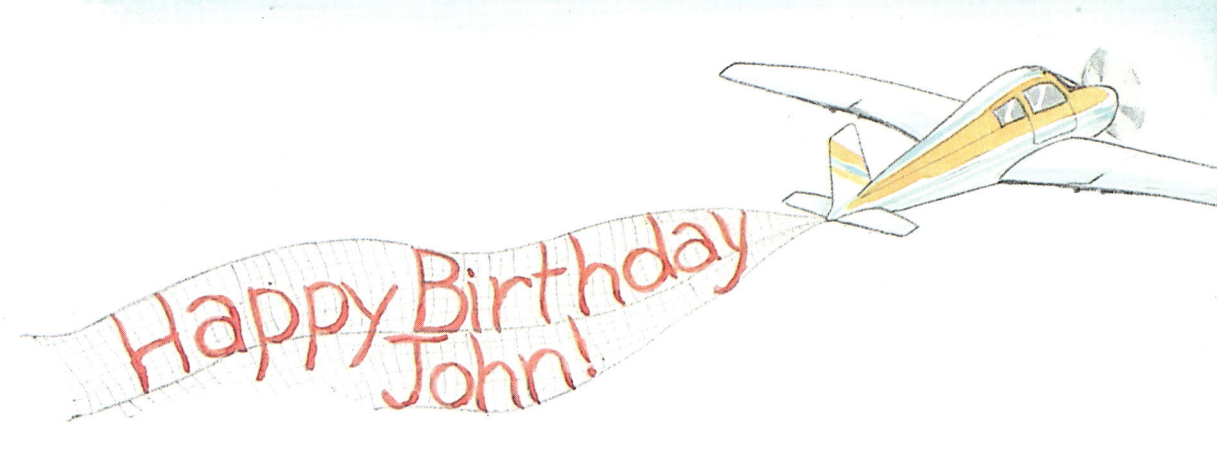

Mother: Look, John!
It's Gramps.

John: What a surprise!
You and my friends are here.
And now Gramps is here, too.
This is a big day for me!

Things That Go

This can fly.

This can fly, too.

Can you tell what this is?

42

This is big.

What is in it?

What do you think makes this go?

Would it be fun to go in it?

You can go in this.

But you have to work to make it go.

You can make this go.

This can go, too.
Where can it take you?

What do you see here?
Where do you think it will go?

Skill   Predicting Outcomes
What Will They Do?

Pam wants to get a surprise for Max.
Max would like to have a kite.
What do you think Pam will do?

Fox and Rabbit are not friends.
Fox wants to get Rabbit.
What will Rabbit do?

Fox: Good day, Little Rabbit.
Can a frog get some lunch here?

Rabbit: A frog can get a good lunch.
Are you a frog?

Fox: Do I look like a frog?

Rabbit: You look like a frog to me.
You look like a big red frog!

Fox: May I come in for my lunch?

Rabbit: I will see.

I will tell Mother you are here.

Mother will make lunch for you.

Fox: OK, Little Rabbit.

That will do for now.

Rabbit: Mother! Mother!
A big red frog wants to come in.

Mother: A red frog?

Rabbit: Yes, Mother, a big red frog.
The frog wants some lunch.

Mother: Frogs aren't red!
Tell me, Little Rabbit.
Did the frog have a tail?

Rabbit: Yes, Mother, a big red tail.

Mother: That is not a frog!
That is a fox!

Rabbit: Look at this, Mother.
Fox wants rabbits for lunch!
What will we do?

Mother: You will see, Little Rabbit.
Fox will get a lunch.
But it will not be rabbits.
Fox is in for a big surprise!

Fox: Good day, Mother Rabbit.

May I come in for some lunch?

Mother: No, you may not come in.

But I do have some lunch for you.

You may have it out here.

Fox: OK, Mother Rabbit.

That will have to do for now.

Mother: Do you like your lunch?

Fox: Yes, this is good!
What is it?

Mother: It's what frogs like for lunch.

Fox: What is that, Mother Rabbit?

Mother: It's fly soup.

Fox: Fly soup?

Mother: Yes, would you like more soup?

Fox: No! No! No!
I do not want more fly soup!
I have to go home now.

Rabbit: Your fly soup did it, Mother! Look at that fox go!

Reading Helps

Sounds You Know

b c d f g h
j k l m n p
r s t v w y

th

___ d ___ g ___ k

___ n ___ r ___ t

New Sounds

fl fr ch

___ x ___ p ___ th ___ ch